DIANA STURM

Young, Fabulous & Broke

Basic Budgeting for the Bad Ass Generation

First published by CopperFire Digital, LLC 2024

Cover design: Diana Sturm

Cover template provided by © Roksolana Fursa via Canva.com

Cataloging-in-Publication Data is on file at the Library of Congress.

Paperback ISBN: 979-8-9900683-0-8

E-book ISBN: 979-8-99000683-1-5

First edition

This book was professionally typeset on Reedsy.
Find out more at reedsy.com

Contents

Introduction

Welcome to Young, Fabulous & Broke: Basic Budgeting for the Bad-Ass Generation. My name is Diana Sturm and I'm excited to be writing this book. As a licensed professional counselor, I work with a lot of young adults who are struggling financially. They worry about their income and rising expenses. They wonder if they'll ever be able to move out of their parent's home or buy any type of property. Most have never been shown how to set up a budget and what factors to consider when reviewing both their income and expenses.

You may wonder what type of experience a counselor has in budgeting. A brief background about myself: my undergraduate degree was in business and I worked for several years doing tax preparation, financial planning, and insurance consultations for individuals and small businesses. I now run my own separate businesses for trauma therapy, educational trainings for individuals and therapists, and confidence coaching.

This book is not the definitive book for managing your money because there are many different components for you to consider and another book may be more useful for your specific situation. This book is just a **first** step in learning how to manage your money. Once you have the ability to meet your expenses and save, you can start investing. There are many other books to lead you through the investing process. This book does not discuss investing.

This book will provide you with a solid foundation for tracking your income and expenses along with points to consider for each category. I will ask you to consider your emotions because emotions do play a BIG role in how we manage finances. Not considering these points can lead to greater financial stress or even financial ruin. (Don't worry, while financial ruin is not good, it doesn't last forever).

This book also asks you to take action. I am going to show you how to create a basic budget and what to include on that budget sheet. This book asks you to create a budget for your income and expenses for one month.

Let's Get Started!

Bad Ass & Broke

Social media scrolls
Influencers
Ballers & Moneybags
Targeted Marketing
Algorithms

Our world feels overwhelming. We are bombarded on media by companies and influencers asking us to buy products, look a certain way, act a certain way, or have a certain lifestyle. We are told by society that the end-all-be-all is to be rich.

The reality is that most people don't have a lot of money and many people are struggling. Their expenses are higher than their income and their goals of living the good life feel out of reach. They feel stuck and don't know how to move forward.

Many people share their dreams with others and find that other people will tell them to scale back their dreams or in some cases to give up their dreams entirely. There are also people who will make promises to you, telling you they can help you reach your dreams if you just pay them a certain amount and they'll invest it for you. You know you can't trust everyone and that scammers lurk around every corner.

One of the first steps to being more Bad Ass and less Broke is to own responsibility for yourself and your finances.

YOU are 100% responsible for your finances.

Being responsible means you have the power to say "no" or to say "yes". Let's practice saying that aloud a few times: "I have the power to say no or to say yes."

How does that feel?

Successful people are comfortable using "no" and "yes". If you are uncomfortable saying "no" to people, then that is a skill which should be practiced more. There are many resources available to help you get more comfortable with creating boundaries with people and feeling confident saying "no". (Check out the resources section for a couple!)

Why is saying "no" important when discussing finances?

Because you are going to have a lot of people telling you how to spend YOUR money. Those people don't know your goals, your motivation for those goals, or your values. But they will see the money you have and will want you to spend it the way THEY want to spend it. These people might be in your own family or they may be professionals selling services or products. The ability to say "no" will keep you on track to reach your goals.

Being responsible means you can set goals and work towards them. If you have support from family or friends to help you reach your goals, that is great. But if you don't, you can continue moving forward on your own and network to find others with similar goals for emotional support. You might want to check out the FIRE movement (Financial Independence Retire Early). This movement has the goal of gaining financial independence and retiring early by prioritizing extreme saving and investing. Of course, at the core of this idea is having a budget.

Being responsible means you control your life. It means not blaming other people or situations for what happens to you. It means if you are blocked from moving towards your goals in one direction that you learn to pivot and find a new way to reach your goals. It means being able to let go of old goals to establish new, better goals. It means you will face setbacks (because we all have them) but your determination will not allow you to give up.

Each person defines success differently. Some people want to have their own 3 bedroom, 2 bath home in the suburbs. Others want a penthouse in a big city. Still others want a little cabana on the beach in Costa Rica. Each person will have different paths to reach their goals. Some people will find reaching their goals very easy because they already have a good job or transferable skills. Other people will be more challenged reaching for their goals because they may still be looking for the right job or right business. The key to actually becoming Bad Ass and Successful is:

Persistence

You may have heard of the story about the tortoise and the hare. They were going to have a race against each other and the hare was convinced that he was going to win the race because he was fast. The race started and both moved forward. The tortoise was slower than the hare, but she moved at the same pace through the entire race. She was persistent and she kept steadily moving forward. The hare had a different strategy. He started running, but got distracted. He stopped and started again.

Then he stopped again. He was still moving towards the finish line, but the distractions pulled his focus away frequently. Eventually, the tortoise crossed the finish line first and the hare came in second.

Many people will tell you that the moral of the story is "slow and steady wins the race." But another perspective is that both the tortoise and the hare succeeded. They crossed the finish line and made it to their goal. They succeeded because each used the skills that suited them individually. There isn't just one way to financial success, there are as many ways as there are different types of people. Keep coming back to your financial goals – even if you get delayed or diverted. Learn to pivot and you will reach them.

What is a Financial Bad Ass?

Being a Financial Bad Ass means you are unshakable in your finances and your financial goals. It means you have a solid, strong, financial foundation. Having that foundation gives you the confidence and power to move ahead towards bigger goals.

What is a foundation?

For every building, the part of the building that touches the Earth is called the foundation. On top of that foundation, the rest of the building is constructed whether it is one story or twenty stories tall. The foundation has to be strong to support the weight of the building above it. A twenty story building needs a stronger and bigger foundation than a one story building. Where the foundation is placed is also very important. If a building is placed on a rock base or very solid soils, then the foundation will be strong and it won't move or break. If the foundation is placed on loose soils or sand, the soil and sand can wash away from under the foundation and the foundation can crack and break apart. An example of this is visible after a hurricane hits a coastal area. After hurricane Ivan in 2004, there was a multistory building in coastal Alabama that had all of the sand washed out from under the foundation. Because the foundation was gone, the entire building had to be torn down and rebuilt.

A strong financial foundation is one that will take the weight of the experiences that life brings to you. It will support you even when times are bad. Buildings have different sizes and need different types of foundations to support their sizes, people need different types of foundations too. A young single person who only has to be responsible for themselves would need a different foundation than a family with three children under the age of five. The family needs a bigger, stronger foundation because there are more people relying on it. A budget can help create the foundation for a strong financial future. A budget is an accounting of income taken in each month and how that money is spent.

Continuing financial education

If you want to become a Financial Bad Ass, after creating your budget and really understanding how the different components make up your financial picture, you will need to continue your financial education. This education will need to be individualized for your specific goals. Some people may want to invest in real estate or in building their own businesses. Other people will use the stock market as their primary investments. Each of these investments are entire fields of knowledge that require continued education. You don't have to become an expert in these fields, but you need to learn enough to make informed decisions that affect your money.

Take Action

Let's get started on creating a budget individualized for you. The ease of creating your budget will vary depending on how confident you are in your current financial situation. But don't worry. We are going to start slow, I'm here by your side, and we are going to take it one step at a time.

To start:

Check in with how you are feeling right now. What emotions are you having?

Many people are terrified to look at their finances. Just today I saw someone on social media say they were afraid to do their taxes because they thought they might owe money to the government. While getting audited by the government may feel scary, it is something that can be faced with confidence. I know, I've been audited and I'm still alive today! Fear about finances can also stop people from doing many things from reaching for their dreams of going to college to starting a family or a business. Fear even stops many people from learning the basics about their finances. Fear is what keeps people from taking action.

It's time to face that fear.

No matter how bad you might think your finances are today, you can improve them. Knowing what you have in terms of income and expenses is the first step. When you know your numbers, you have nothing to fear. Numbers are solid and concrete. You can hold dollars, pounds, and euros in your hands. When you know your numbers, you know what you have, and you can make decisions based on those numbers.

Today we will look at your numbers by completing a budget. This includes numbers for your income and your expenses. At this point, we don't need a calculator, but in a few chapters you will need one. (Hint: there's a calculator on your phone.)

Budget Time Frame

Budgets can be created for any period of time and longer time periods are used for businesses and governments. These large organizations have one year or even longer budgets. For individuals and families, one month is chosen because most bills are paid monthly. This book covers how to create a budget for one month.

What you need:

Digital or Paper?

First, choose how you want to keep your budget. Do you want to use your computer or a sheet of paper. It's your choice. Sometimes when I create documents on my computer, they get lost in the void and I forget about them. So for things I want to keep in my current focus, I will use paper and I will keep that paper on my desk where I can see it and be reminded that I need to take action. Having your budget readily available and in sight can help you make more informed purchasing decisions.

You will need one sheet of paper or one open document. If you are using a computer, eventually, you may want to switch to a spreadsheet program to track your budget over time. Many people track their income growth, investments, and reduction of debts. Some people make fancy spreadsheets and keep them for years. But for right now, you just need a single document page.

Step 1: Create a budget page. On a sheet of paper or computer document, write down the following headings at the top of the page: My Budget with the month written underneath. Then divide the page into left and right columns. The left column should have the heading "Income" and the right column should have the heading "Expenses."

My Budget (insert month)	
Income	Expenses

Good job on the first step!

Income

Income is defined as the money you receive. Income includes money from:

- a job
- a side hustle
- a business
- a variety of investments
- disability payments
- social security
- a trust, or
- lottery winnings.

Income could be received daily, weekly, monthly, or yearly. It is money that can be deposited into a bank or that you can spend. Most income is also taxable. Income is the most important factor in creating your financial foundation.

No income means no foundation.

The average person has at least one job. If the person works at this job fulltime, more than 35 hours a week, we can consider this their primary income. If that income is not enough to pay for the expenses, many people get additional jobs or start side hustles. A side hustle is a business you run outside of your primary job. Second jobs or side hustles can often take up as much time as the primary job.

When people are establishing themselves after high school, trade school or college, their sole source of income will come from a primary job along with other part-time jobs or side hustles. This time period is great for forming a stable financial foundation. But if you are farther along in your career, that is fine too. Learning how to create a budget is helpful for anyone at any age to better manage their finances.

Gross income is the total amount of income received during a specific time period before deductions are taken out. When a person is hired for a job, a salary or hourly wage is exchanged for work. The salary or hourly wage is gross income. Typical deductions include government taxes including income tax and social security, health and life insurance offered by the employer, and savings plans for retirement. Taxes are required, insurance and savings are often optional.

Net income is the amount of pay you receive after deductions have been taken out.

Gross Income – Deductions = Net Income

Step 2: Gather information on what you are getting paid from all of your jobs, side hustles, and other sources. If you have paystubs look at your paystub and find the net income or net pay amount. If you have a direct deposit to your bank, get the exact number that is being deposited each pay period. The net income is the amount you get to take home and spend.

Net Income = Amount You Can Spend

How many hours does your paystub cover? One week? Two weeks? One month? Is your check the same every pay period or does it change? Is there a minimum amount it never goes under?

For instance, if you work in retail and receive hourly pay, one week you may work 35 hours and the next week you may work 38 hours. There will be a slight difference in the pay between the weeks. If you never go under 35 hours, but each week there is some variance, for the budget we will calculate based on the 35 hours.

For a one month budget, if you get paid:

Weekly: Multiply the weekly number by 4, then enter into budget

Every other week: Multiply the biweekly number by 2, then enter into budget

Monthly: Enter the number straight into the budget.

Example:

Sarina has 3 jobs. One pays monthly, one weekly and one every other week. She would calculate them like this:

Job 1 (monthly) $1,700.00. She enters $1,700.00.

Job 2 (weekly) $375.00. $375 x 4 = $1,500.00. She would enter $1,500.00.

Job 3 (biweekly) $350.00. $350 x 2 = $700.00. She would enter $700.00.

Sarina's weekly job has different hours each week. One week she may have $275, the next $430, the next $395, and the next $410. Her average pay is $377.50. [Average pay = ($275.00 + $430.00 + $395.00 + $410.00) divided by 4]. Sarina has decided to use $375 a week as her average for budgeting. She may have some months where she has more money from her weekly job than she budgeted for, that's great. She can choose how she wants to use that "extra" money later to pay a bill, to put into emergency savings, or to save for a future purchase like a car or vacation.

Enter your **NET** income, not your gross income.

Step 3: Enter your income on the left side of your budget page under the Income heading. List each job separately, full time job, part time job, and savings. If you have more jobs, list them separately.

My Budget May			
Income		Expenses	
Full time Job	$2,200		
Part time Job Savings	$400 $1.05		
Total			

This example is for a person with one full time job, one part time job, and a basic savings account. Basic savings accounts don't pay much interest but they are good to hold emergency funds.

Needs vs Wants

One of the biggest sources of confusion for people is recognizing the difference between what is a need versus what is a want. Many publications describe needs vs wants as an either or choice. They often visualize the concept with a scale where one arm is holding wants and the other is holding needs:

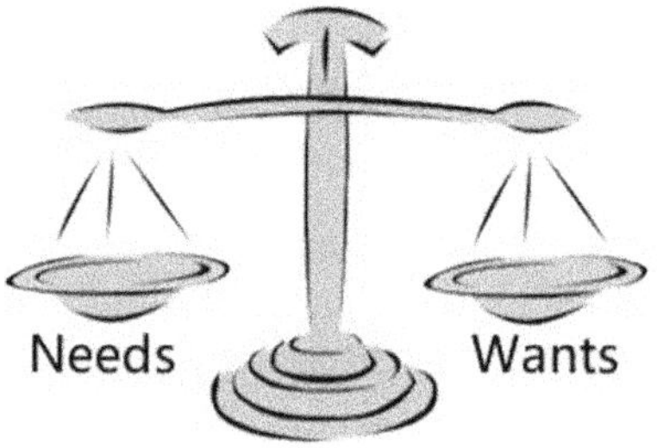

The scales imply there is nothing in between and a person has to make a choice between needs and wants. But in reality, wants are in addition to our needs. A more realistic representation would be to represent needs and wants as a bar graph where there is a short bar on the left and the bars increase in size when moving to the right.

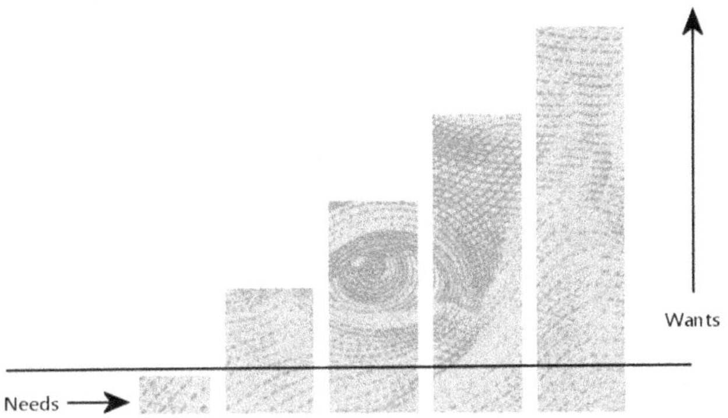

Each person has a base level of needs. Above that is wants.

The shortest bar on the graph represents the base level of needs. Moving to the right on the graph shows an increase in a person's level of income. When income increases, a person can start to purchase or satisfy their wants. Needs are shown at the bottom because needs have to be met before wants can be added.

What is a need?

A need is something a person needs for survival.

Food

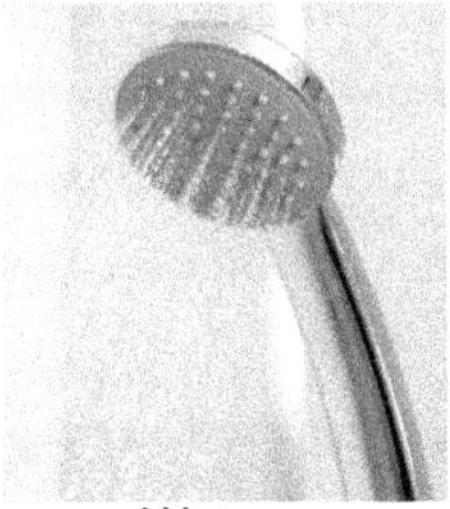

Water

Shelter

Every person needs food, water, and shelter. Food and water nourish our bodies and shelter protects us from outside elements like rain, snow, and temperature extremes. Most people don't think about needs until a disaster strikes. Earthquakes, hurricanes, blizzards, tornadoes, and floods can all take away these basic needs. Even financial ruin can take these away. For people in areas hit by by one of these, a direct impact can mean living for days or weeks without electricity. Having water, food, and a roof over your head means you were one of the lucky people who made it through the disaster. Life can bring all types of experiences of disaster but covering these basic needs plus some extended basic needs is more important than anything else. Not having the basics of food, water, and shelter is emotionally draining and can lead to pervasive feelings of sadness.

Many people barely earn enough money to pay for basic needs. In addition, prices keep rising for these needs. In large metro areas, like New York or Tokyo, rents are very high even for a tiny apartment. Many people have small one room studio apartments which cost thousands of dollars each month. At the time of writing this book, the lowest price small one room studio apartment with one bathroom in Manhattan, New York, New York, costs $1,600 per month. If rent is 1/3 of net income, then the renter would need to earn at least $4,800 per month net after paying taxes. In low cost of living areas, the same amount of money each month can rent large apartments, rent houses, or even purchase small houses. In some regions of the U.S., $1,600 a month can rent a 3 bedroom, 2 bath renovated house, no utilities included.

The cost of basic needs will vary by location.

The more people you need to support, the more expensive the basic needs will be. Within each of the categories of food, water, and shelter, there can be huge variations in what people spend. One person might eat a bowl of rice or oatmeal while another person eats steak and seafood. As more income comes in, a person can improve their food choices and food quality. More income can mean using bottled water instead of tap water. More income can mean moving up from a small apartment to a bigger apartment or moving from a less safe neighborhood to a more safe neighborhood.

Extended Basic Needs

Note also, there are things which are not included in basic needs survival, but that qualify as needs. These are extended basic needs and they include: transportation, electricity, cell phones, and internet service. Extended basic needs are variable costs which can be adjusted up or down depending on available income. When money gets tight, these extended basic needs can be reduced and added back in later. Cars can be given up for public transportation, heat can be turned down and lights turned off to reduce electricity use, free Wi-Fi in public areas can be used with cell phones and for internet service.

Wants

A want is anything that can be purchased that is not a need. Wants include

- Clothing & Personal Care Items
- Furniture & Decorations
- Entertainment including restaurants, movies, streaming services, music & sporting events
- Cars
- Bigger homes

- Vacations
- Materials for Hobbies
- Games & Devices
- Spending money on special events including birthdays, holidays, and weddings

Being able to identify the difference between a want and a need is important because wants can be delayed until more money is available to pay for a purchase in cash. A high percentage of what people spend money on is wants.

Examples of Needs vs Wants:

Need: Transportation

Want: Much Nicer Transportation

When looking at transportation, we need to be able to move to different places for work or to shop. Public transportation will satisfy this need. A want for transportation is having your own car or truck. This want may range from a small inexpensive car to a top of the line luxury truck. The need is transportation, the want is having very nice transportation.

Need: Basic Kitchen

Want: Gourmet Kitchen

Another need is having a basic kitchen. A basic kitchen would include a source of water, some source of heat for cooking and a place which is cool to keep foods for longer periods of time. A want is having a gourmet kitchen with top of the line appliances and cooking tools.

Ideas for wants are planted in people from family, friends, and society. For many individuals social pressure drives their wants. People are pressured into "having the right image", the "right lifestyle", or "having the wedding of their dreams." But their income doesn't come close to providing those things for them and they start to borrow money by using credit cards or even worse, taking out home equity loans to pay for wants. The loans from credit cards and equity loans result in increasing loan balances and increasing monthly payments. These increasing monthly payments cause huge emotional stress. Many years ago I met a woman who complained endlessly about her husband. She reported she had been married for 15 years and hated him. I asked her why she stayed married. She said, "My parents took out a second mortgage on their house so I could have a dream wedding and they are still paying for it." Fifteen years later, still in debt, and miserable.

Social media and advertising are designed to get you to buy more and more products. It's very easy for money to be spent on wants. Learning how to say "no" to social pressure and waiting to pay for wants with cash is the goal. With each purchase, ask yourself, "Is this a need or a want?" and that question should be followed up with, "Do I have cash to pay for this?" These questions are much easier to answer if you know how much money is available to spend on wants. This is where the practice of keeping a monthly budget becomes very important.

Expenses

Income is received and then it can be spent on expenses. Expenses are anything that can be purchased with money. This could be gas for your car, a visit to the doctor, rent for an apartment, or a trip that's on your bucket list. Income limits the amount of money that can be spent without going into debt.

Your income will limit the amount you can spend.

Controlling expenses is an important part of creating a stable foundation. Controlling expenses and learning how to manage and then grow your money means that in the future, you could pay cash for a car or a vacation and not need to take out a loan from a bank or your credit cards. How great would it feel to go to Hawaii and know that everything was paid in advance? It would feel very different from going to Hawaii and charging everything on credit cards then receiving the bills two weeks after you return from your trip. Credit card bills begin to feel like a ball and chain that gets heavier and heavier over time. The Financial Bad Ass is going to have the vacation paid in advance and really enjoy the vacation without any worry about paying for it later.

What do you want? Ball & Chain? Or Financial Bad Ass?

Step 4: Create a list of all expenses. This is where the money is spent each month. Some people like to carry a small notebook and write down all of the times they spend money during the day. This method is good if you use cash for purchases. Other people use a debit or credit card for everything and can pull their bank statements to see how much they have spent. Include ALL items you put on your credit cards too. To create a budget, we will be looking at two types of expenses: fixed and variable.

Fixed Expenses

A **fixed expense** is the same amount every month. These include:

Rent/Mortgage
Car payment
Health insurance
Student loans
Some utilities

Fixed expenses don't have any flexibility. These are flat amounts paid every month. For fixed expenses, it is common practice to review the ratio of fixed expenses to your monthly income. Why? Because overspending can occur for fixed expenses too. The ratio is the cost of the fixed expense divided by the net income.

Cost of Fixed Expense / Net Income = % Ratio

Most published guidelines use gross income to determine this, but people don't get to take home gross income. People take home net income after taxes and insurance. It makes more sense to **use net income** because that is the actual money you have available in your hands to spend.

Ratios are flexible and are not carved in stone. For people making $50,000 and under, you might need to spend more on fixed expenses and for people who earn more than $50,000 you might spend a lot less on fixed expenses. You want to have the ratios in mind so you don't hit a danger zone for spending.

What is a spending danger zone?

It is when one expense item on your budget takes up the majority of your income. In an ideal world, no single expense would take more than 25% of your net income. The higher your income, the easier this is to achieve.

Net income target ratios:

Rent – 50% or less. 25% or less is your goal. Get paying roommates or find a lower cost location. Remember the saying about real estate: Location, location, location. In big cities, the rent can drop by just moving one block away from a desirable area. Being on a lake or waterfront will cost more than being across the street from the lake or waterfront.

Mortgage – 50% or less. 25% or less is your goal. Get paying roommates, banks will often accept a lease agreement from someone who wants to move in with you if you purchase the property. They will include this rent as additional income when calculating what you can afford. Keep in mind that just because a bank says you can afford a certain amount, doesn't mean you should spend that amount. Could you still afford this house if you had a big pay cut? Houses are long term commitments, keep your payments as low as possible. Another big factor no one tells you is that if you get a fixed mortgage, the bank pays the house insurance and property taxes as part of the payment package. The monthly payment will NOT stay fixed over time. Why? Because insurance and taxes go up as the property value increases. Your income is not guaranteed to go up. Get a house you can easily afford now.

Remember the cost for shelter is a **NEED**. This expense **must** be covered by your income. The lower your cost for shelter, the more money you will have available for other expenses. Shelter is normally the largest expense for people.

Car payment – 13% or less. Living in a big metro area with good public transportation? A car often isn't needed. There are a lot of additional expenses which must be included in the cost of a car: maintenance, gas/batteries, insurance, and parking costs. In many areas, a parking space can cost hundreds of dollars a month to rent. If a car is necessary, the cost for the car should be less than 13% of your monthly income. The best way to reduce the cost is to save money for a downpayment on a car. While cars do have value, they are considered what is called a "depreciating asset." That means after a car is purchased, the value of the car goes down. This is the opposite of what a house or other real estate is considered. A house is considered a "non-depreciating asset" meaning that over a period of time, if properly maintained, its value will either stay the same or go up. The higher the downpayment on a car, the lower the monthly payment. There are also a huge variety of cars, so it is easy to purchase a car based on what you can afford.

Many people cave into "wants" when it comes to purchasing cars and overspend to get a car that projects an image they want of themselves. This is fine if the income is there to support that want. But without the stable financial foundation to pay for the desired car, the financial picture can quickly become very negative and regrets for purchasing the car can quickly set in. How to reduce the car expense? Look into public transportation, lower cost new cars, or gently used cars. **Transportation is an extended basic need** and there are lower cost options. Establish a stable financial foundation with increasing income and you can plan in the future to purchase the car you want.

Student loans – There are two types of student loans, federal loans, and private loans. When there is an option, pay attention to federal loans because they have the most flexibility in repayment plans plus there is always a possibility that the government may forgive portions of those loans. Private loans don't have the same options and are good to consider only after federal loans have been maxed out.

Before taking out student loans - When taking out student loans, be sure they are used only for needs: the cost of tuition, books and other school expenses, or basic needs. Don't spend student loan money on entertainment, restaurants, clothing, personal care, or other consumable wants. Get a job to pay for wants. Do you want to pay for a haircut 10 years after your hair was cut? Using a loan to pay consumables doesn't make sense.

What is a consumable?

Consumables are items that once purchased are used very quickly. A haircut lasts only for a few weeks before the hair needs to be cut again. Food is used right away or within just a few days. These types of expenses should always be paid with cash not credit. (Credit is okay IF you pay the balance in full each month.)

Before taking out student loans, investigate if your employer has any options which might help to pay for education. Some employers offer to pay for one or two classes each term as an employee benefit. When I went back to school for my Master's degree, I was working at a school and they offered tuition reimbursement for two classes each term. I had to pay for the class before taking it, then when the class was finished, I submitted the bill along with my final grades for the class. If the grades were Cs or above, the employer reimbursed me for the cost of the classes.

Some employers will ask that a certain type of degree is earned, for instance some hospitals will pay for a nursing education if the person signs a contract that they will work at the hospital for a certain number of years after they become a registered nurse. For the trades, instead of going to a technical school, investigate training offered by unions or the state department of labor. Unions often have formal training programs where a person starts as an apprentice then moves up to journeyman, and eventually a master in the trade. As much as possible, reduce the amount needed for student loans.

Repayment of student loans - For all types of student loan repayment, explore all of the options presented. In particular, look for Income Based Repayment plans. These types of plans will look at your income tax returns and present options to you based on your income.

For undergraduate loans, the typical repayment is 5% of income. For graduate loans, the typical repayment is 10% of income.

Options change over time and for federal loans, the payment option can be changed once a year. New options might be more beneficial to your specific situation. It is good practice to understand the loan repayment options and to review them annually. This is true for all loans held.

Health insurance - In the United States, health insurance is quite expensive so many people look for jobs which offer reduced cost or free health insurance as an employee benefit. Shopping around for insurance is very important because there are dramatic differences in cost and in what is covered under different health insurance plans. One of the best places to start looking is the government Marketplace. You can get assistance in choosing a plan and based on your income, there may be discounts for the cost of coverage. The most important factor to consider is that high deductible plans require you to have a large amount of money in savings to cover that deductible. I have seen many people with insurance not get medical care because they could not afford the deductible.

Totaling fixed expenses - Ratio Goals

There may be other fixed expenses that were not included in this list. But let's take a look at how much we've spent just on the fixed expenses. The numbers you have may be higher or lower than these. These percentages are based on net income. Lower ratios for fixed expenses is better.

Rent/mortgage 25% - 50%
Car payment 10% - 15%
Health insurance 0% – 20%
Student loans 5% - 10%
Totals 40% - 95%

Read those numbers very carefully. 40% to 95% of your net income could be going to fixed expenses! As you increase your income, the ratio of the amounts you are paying for fixed expenses will go down and more income can be spent on variable expenses. Not having a car payment or student loans will reduce your fixed expenses.

Example:

Net monthly income:

	Person A	Person B	Person C
Monthly Income	$4,000	$5,000	$6,000
Rent	$1,600	$1,600	$1,600
Ratio	40%	32%	26%
	No!	Better	Best

This example only uses one item from the fixed expenses, rent. There are three people with the same amount of rent, but they have different incomes. The first person has $4,000 a month income, the second has $5,000 a month income and the third, $6,000 a month income. All are paying $1,600 a month in rent. When the ratio is calculated, for the first person $1,600 divided by $4,000 = 40%. The ratio for the second person is 32%, and for the third person the ratio is 26%. This example illustrates how increasing income while keeping the fixed expenses the same means the ratio for fixed expenses will go down. More money is available for variable expenses. The third person who is earning $6,000 a month while paying $1,600 for rent is in a much more stable financial position because they have the lowest ratio for shelter. The goal is to reduce the ratios for fixed expenses.

Percentages are used in this book because each person and each location will have different income levels and different costs for expenses. When looking at income, the income before spending is 100%. Nothing has been spent and you still hold all of your income. Fixed expenses will take a certain percentage of your income. The actual costs will vary dramatically from location to location and from person to person. Costs in New York City are going to be much higher than in Agra, Kansas. To find a percentage, take the expense and divide it by the income.

Expense / Income = % Ratio

If spending is more than 100% of income, then money must be borrowed to pay for the spending. The goal is to have a high enough income to pay for all expenses without borrowing.

Maximum	100%
Fixed Expense Total	40 - 95%
Available for Variable Expenses	5 – 60%

If the maximum is 100% and the fixed expenses range from 40 to 95% of the maximum, only 5 to 60% of the money will be available for variable expenses. Clearly having 95% of income used for fixed expenses will not work, you will need more money for the variable expenses. Fixed expenses must be reduced.

Example:

	Person A	Person B
Net Income	$4,000	$4,000
Fixed Expenses	40%	95%
Fixed Expenses in $$	$1,600	$3,800
$$ Available for variable expenses	$2,400	$200

Both Person A and Person B receive the same income each month, $4,000. Person A has lower fixed expenses of 40%, or $1,600, and will have more money available for variable expenses, $2,400. This person may have enough money to begin creating an emergency fund or saving for a bigger purchase. Person B has high fixed expenses of 95%, or $3,800, and will not have enough money available for variable expenses, only $200. This person will have to borrow money and will go into debt just to purchase the basic variable expenses such as clothing or personal care items. Person B will not be able to establish an emergency savings account or save for big purchases.

Goal: Keep fixed expenses low

Variable Expenses

Variable expenses change each month and can include unexpected purchases. These include payments for:

Utility bills like electricity, water, cell phones, TV, and internet
Food
Medical – doctor, dentist, optometrist
Clothing
Personal care – haircuts, massages, skin care
Hobbies
Entertainment – restaurants, clubs, sporting events
Variable Debt - Credit cards (more on those later)

Variable expenses are the expenses you have the most control over. You can increase or reduce these expenses from month to month. Many people lower their heat in the winter to save money on their heating bills or raise the temperature in the summer to save electricity on their air conditioning bills. Other people will cook at home and eat lower cost foods to save money. Other people will wait an extra week or two to get a haircut or decide not to purchase new clothes this season to reduce expenses.

Variable expenses need to stay within the income left over after fixed expenses have been paid. Variable expenses can eat up that income very fast. For our example of a person taking home $4000 a month, after fixed expenses, the money remaining could be as low as $200 to a maximum of $2,400 a month.

Utility bills can easily run $300 to $500 a month
Food – conservatively, $300 - $500 a month
Haircuts - $40 - $60 a month
Entertainment – restaurants twice a week @ $20 a meal = $160 a month
Total so far $800 - $1,220

What if something comes up? A trip to Urgent Care, car maintenance, new clothing for a job interview, or a special occasion like a wedding or birthday. Credit card bills have to be paid too. The $200 to $2,400 a month will disappear very quickly. This is why it is very important to know where you stand financially. Track your expenses to help you decide how and where to spend your money. Learn to say "no" to yourself and other people if you do not have the money to do something.

Exploring "No"

Let's take a minute to explore saying "no" to yourself and others. What feelings come up when thinking about saying "no"? Many people were not taught how to set boundaries with other people or for themselves so saying "no" can be scary. Where is the fear coming from? Fear of upsetting another person? Fear of being rejected? What about saying "no" to yourself?

A budget is a type of boundary that you are defining for yourself. It tells you when to stop spending to avoid going into debt. It means you will have to tell yourself "no" because money won't always be available for purchases. No's can lead to good things. No's about spending money can lead to more purchases with cash instead of credit, more money left over after expenses, more emergency savings, more investments, more financial freedom. More Bad Ass and less broke. Be willing to say "no" to others and yourself. Repeat this phrase to yourself: "I have a budget I am sticking to. Sticking to it will lead to financial stability."

Money saved from reducing variable expenses can be saved for specific purposes. These savings can be used for emergencies, for downpayments for bigger purchases including homes and cars, for investments like the purchase of a business, or for retirement savings. These types of savings provide financial stability and allow for future financial growth and success. This is the level where you become a Financial Bad Ass.

Credit cards/credit scores

The fact is that the U.S. economy uses credit. Since 1989, a system has monitored individuals and judged each person based on how they are using credit and has assigned them a credit score. If the model determines a person is using credit wisely, they will have a high credit score, but if the model determines the person is using credit poorly, they will be assigned a low credit score. Credit scores can change over time and go up or go down.

Low credit scores can also come from not using credit at all and paying cash for everything. For people who pay cash, their credit scores can be low resulting in the same problems as for people who don't use credit wisely.

Credit scores are determined by monitoring five factors:

- Payment history – Do you pay monthly bills on time every time?
- Credit history length – The longer credit is open and managed wisely, the more favorable lenders see you.
- Total amount owed – When a line of credit is opened, do not use the entire amount. Keep the amount used as low as possible. Lenders look at the ratio of the amount of credit available to the amount of credit used.
- Credit utilization – Refers to the number of accounts held and how often inquiries are made about your credit score. If you are renting an apartment or buying a house, your credit score will be checked and this is considered a "hard" inquiry. Too many of these types of hard inquiries within a certain period of time can reduce your credit score. Having too many credit cards is also seen as a negative by lenders even though lenders bombard consumers with credit card offers daily.
- Diverse credit portfolio – Having a variety of types of credit is also important. This means having fixed and variable loans. Mortgages, car payments, and student loans are fixed and credit cards are variable. Having one mortgage, one car payment, one department store credit card and one major credit card which is accepted anywhere is a good example of a diverse credit portfolio.

Keeping a high credit score reaps benefits including lowered insurance costs, better housing opportunities for renting, better interest rates to borrow money for cars, homes, and credit cards.

For those who pay cash for purchases, which is a good practice, it is a good idea to establish and maintain credit. This can be as simple as paying for a low cost item every couple of months with a credit card and then paying it off in a couple of days. If you stop using credit cards and stop making small purchases, the accounts will be closed after a certain period of time, often six months to a year. Once closed, that line of credit will not be available to you.

Low credit scores have penalties including the inability to rent, purchase cars or homes, and higher insurance costs. If you are allowed to do these things, a low credit score will often mean extra security deposits or high interest rates on your purchases.

How to get credit and a credit score? - Short answer: You have to borrow money and then pay it off. There are several options to establishing credit. The first is to go to a bank or credit union and talk with a banker about establishing credit. The bank may require a basic checking or savings account to be opened. The bank or credit union may offer either a low secured credit account or an unsecured credit account. A secured credit card means a certain amount of money must be deposited into an account and left there, then the bank would issue a credit card with a credit limit for the same amount of money that was deposited. For instance, the banker may ask you to deposit $500 and then the bank will give you a credit card with a $500 credit limit. The $500 that was deposited must stay in the account for the entire time the credit card is active so that money cannot be spent. An unsecured credit card does not require a deposit as a condition for getting a line of credit. Unsecured credit cards will have lower credit limits until the borrower proves they can use credit wisely and pay it off.

Another option many people use is to open a credit card with a retail store. The card can only be used at that store and the credit limit will be lower. Often department stores offer credit to those who don't have established credit. The key for all credit accounts opened is that after the purchase is made, it must be paid off on time. This can be broken into several payments or just one payment. If you choose to pay over time, interest will be added for borrowing the money. Find out the due date for payment, and make sure you make at least the minimum monthly payment amount on time.

It takes time to establish credit, months and sometimes even several years. Do you have goals of owning a home or opening a business? Then establishing your credit early is a wise move. Paying off the money borrowed is key to keeping a good credit score.

Completing Your Budget

Is the list of expenses ready? Now those expenses will be added to the budget. On the right side of the budget sheet, all of the individual expenses will be listed, starting with the fixed expenses. List each expense individually do not lump them together.

Step 5: List the fixed expenses first. These are non-negotiable and are the same amount each month.

Step 6: List the variable expenses next. Add as many lines as needed. A blank form is provided in the next section on totaling your budget. The example shows for the month of May fixed expenses of rent of $860 per month, as a roommate; health insurance of $125 from the Marketplace; a bus pass for $75; and student loans of $200. There is a space for totaling the fixed expenses. The variable expenses are listed next and include: food for $470; utilities for $250; personal care for $300; entertainment for $200; and savings of $100. There is a space for totaling the variable expenses. At the bottom of the right side, there is a space for the grand total of all of the fixed and variable expenses.

My Budget May			
Income		Expenses	
Full time Job	$2,200	Fixed Expenses	
Part time Job	$400	Rent/Mortgage	$860 w/ roommates
Savings	$1.05	Health Insurance	$125 Marketplace
		Bus Pass	$75
		Student Loans	$200
		Total Fixed Expenses	
		Variable Expenses	
		Food	$470
		Utilities	$250
		Personal Care	$300
		Entertainment	$220
		Savings	$100
		Total Variable Expenses	
Total		Total Expenses	

Count all money spent within the month including cash, debit cards, credit cards, or other loans.

Totaling Your Budget

Step 7: Total the income column. The example budget has a total for the two jobs and the savings account of $2,601.05.

Step 8: Total the expense column. First total the fixed expenses. Then total the variable expenses. Add the fixed and variable expenses together. The fixed and variable expenses should be totaled separately so the ratios can be reviewed.

Your completed budget sheet should look something like the example. The example shows the total fixed expenses equal $1,260 and the variable expenses equal $1,340. The grand total of all expenses equals $2,600.

Your budget sheet may have more lines and different expenses. A blank budget sheet follows the example.

My Budget May			
Income		Expenses	
Full time Job	$2,200	Fixed Expenses	
Part time Job	$400	Rent/Mortgage	$860 w/ roommates
Savings	$1.05	Health Insurance	$125 Marketplace
		Bus Pass	$75
		Student Loans	$200
		Total Fixed Expenses	$1,260
		Variable Expenses	
		Food	$470
		Utilities	$250
		Personal Care	$300
		Entertainment	$220
		Savings	$100
		Total Variable Expenses	$1,340
Total	$2,601.05	Total Expenses	$2,600

In Step 9, ratios will be examined.

Here is a blank form to make your budget. Add as many rows as you need for income and expenses.

My Budget (Insert Month)			
Income		Expenses	
Job 1		Fixed Expenses	
Job 2		Rent/Mortgage	
Savings		Health Insurance	
		Transportation/ Car Loan/ Bus Pass	
		Student Loans	
		Total Fixed Expenses	
		Variable Expenses	
		Food	
		Utilities	
		Personal Care	
		Entertainment	
		Savings	
		Total Variable Expenses	
Total		Total Expenses	

Step 9: Compare the totals for income & expenses. - These totals will help you make financial decisions for the next month. If you find there are more fixed expenses and the income isn't high enough, then step back and assess how income can be increased. Are there opportunities for promotion in the current job? Are there new jobs being listed that can be applied for? Is the side hustle beginning to bring

in more revenue?

Are fixed expenses within the ratio guidelines? In the budget example, the ratios for the fixed expenses are:

Rent: $860 is **33%** of the total income of $2,601. ($860 /$2601 = 0.33 x 100 = 33%)

Health insurance: $125 is **4.8%** of $2,601. ($125 /$2601 = 0.048 x 100 = 4.8%)

Bus Pass: $75 is **2.8%** of $2,601. ($75 /$2601 = 0.028 x 100 = 2.8%)

Student loans: $200 is 7.7% of $2,601. ($200 /$2601 = 0.077 x 100 = 7.7%)

Total fixed expenses: $1,260, which is **48%** of total income. ($1260 /$2601 = 0.48 x 100 = 48%)

Total fixed expenses under 50% is great! In this example, this person uses public transportation instead of a car. They may be able to reduce their fixed expenses further by exploring income based student loan repayments.

Are the variable expenses too high? Was there an unexpected expense that took more money this month? It's time to take a close look and see where expenses can be cut back. Budgets will change from month to month. In the example, variable expenses total $1,340 which is 51.5% of total income (numbers for this example have been rounded so they don't quite total 100%). Since variable expenses represent a majority of income, this person is able to adjust them if unexpected expenses come up during the month.

Having an understanding and control of your finances will give you more confidence with handling money. Will there be surprises? Of course, that is what life is about. But by reviewing your monthly finances and being able to make adjustments so income is either equal to or more than expenses, you will gain confidence and know that even if life sends you a curve ball, you can face it and get through it.

Summary of Steps

Summary of Steps
Using the example form:

Step 1: Create a budget page

Step 2: Gather information

Step 3: Enter your income

Step 4: Create a list of all expenses

Step 5: List the fixed expenses

Step 6: List the variable expenses

Step 7: Total the income column

Step 8: Total the expenses column. Take note of the totals for fixed vs variable expenses. Calculate the ratios to see if adjustments need to be made.

Step 9: Compare the totals for income and expenses. Examine ratios for fixed expenses.

Step 10: Continue to learn about money. Check out the resources at the end of the book

Income < Expenses

When income is less than expenses, a hard look needs to be taken at both columns. How can income be increased? Can you get a part time job or start a side hustle? Can you get a roommate to share expenses?

How can expenses be decreased? This examination should look at the ratios of fixed expenses to income. What is your ratio for rent or mortgage to income? Does this ratio need to be less? Look at each of the ratios for the fixed expenses and compare them to the target ranges for those ratios.

Next look at your variable expenses. What variable expenses can you reduce? The goal is to reduce expenses to less than or equal to your income.

This assessment can be emotionally difficult for many people. They work hard and feel like they can never get ahead. But acknowledge these emotions and take responsibility for making financial decisions. Keep using a budget each month. Keep looking for opportunities to increase your monthly income.

Income > Expenses

When you reach the point where income is greater than expenses, it is going to be very tempting to spend that excess income on more wants. Savings can lead to investments. Investments can lead to additional sources of monthly income.

But the reality is that when income is tight, it feels good to treat yourself. That's okay. But consider a compromise. If you have any amount of money left at the end of the month, instead of spending all of it on wanted things, take a portion of it, 40 or 50%, and save it. Ask your bank or credit union about opening a savings account and put away the extra. Gradually increase the amount you save as you gain more control over your finances.

What is this savings for? A savings account can be used for many things. It is a good idea to have money set aside for emergencies. Financial pros often recommend saving an amount equal to 3 to 6 months of expenses. Savings can also be used for down payments on cars and houses. Savings can be used for buying or starting a business, paying for educational costs, going on a vacation, or for retirement.

When an emergency saving account is established and fully funded, then the next step is to learn about investing and how to make your money grow.

Special Budgets

The basic process of creating a budget can be applied to special events or purchases. Many people create separate budgets for weddings, vacations, or large purchases. Because these are often large expenses, advance planning is needed. Special events fall under the consumables category in that once the event occurs nothing remains. The best way to plan for these events is to cut some variable expenses and put money aside in a savings account so little or no debt is incurred for the special event. To increase income to pay for special events or purchases, people often get a second job.

While it may be common for some events to receive money as gifts for the occasion, that money should not be used to pay for the special event. It is not the responsibility of guests to pay for the event. If the wants for the dream event are out of reach for the income level, then there are two choices. Either the list of wants needs to be cut down significantly so the current income can cover expenses, or saving for the event needs to take place for a longer period of time.

Persistence

There are no overnight successes. You have now created your first budget and you have an idea of whether adjustments need to be made or if you are managing money well. Knowing where your money goes and purposely directing it to different areas can help you create a stable foundation. This can grow into investing opportunities and lead towards financial success. You will gain confidence in handling money and in making choices about how to spend it. Continue to learn about managing money.

As you explore your finances, different and sometimes unpleasant emotions might pop up. Don't hide your emotions, but explore them. Write them down. Ask yourself where they came from? Are they messages from your parents or grandparents? Are they from your own life experiences? Do you want to keep these emotions and messages?

Persistence is the key to long term stability and financial success. Still afraid of looking at your financial numbers? Keep learning about money management and keep moving forward. Getting experience and continuing to learn and apply what you learn can move that fear out of your life. If you feel you have bigger emotional blocks, consider seeking help for specific needs. Maybe a career counselor could help. Maybe a mental health counselor could help. Persistence can also mean taking a step forward when you really don't feel like it.

Here are some resources (additional ones for investing are in the resource section)

Mental Health

In the U.S. call or text 988 for the national suicide hotline. Someone is always there to talk to you. For additional resources, visit https://988lifeline.org.

Peer support hotlines are for talking about anything and are available in many states. Seach on the internet for "peer support in (name of your state)".

NAMI, the National Alliance on Mental Illness provides support groups and additional resources. https://www.nami.org/home

Career Counseling

Career Centers from your state's Department of Labor. Search for the Department of Labor in your state and see if there is a career center near you. They offer career advice and opportunities for training; some training is free.

Employment Agencies. Employment agencies receive a commission from corporations for recruiting people to fill job positions. Employment agencies can fill permanent or temporary positions. Often they will offer basic training in various office programs for word processing and basic accounting. Check around to see what is offered in your area.

Conclusion

Congratulations! You have done a lot of things: created your first budget, learned about needs vs wants, learned how to recognize dangerous spending, and you've learned that sometimes the only way to spend what you want is to raise your income levels. You've taken the first steps to becoming a Financial Bad Ass and you've created the outline for a stable foundation.

Make a budget every month and follow it. As your income increases and your expenses decrease, open a savings account. Continue to learn about managing your money. This book gave you the first step in your financial journey and hopefully a push to continue to have persistence to become a Financial Bad Ass.

I knew you could do it! Great job!

If you found this book to be helpful, I'd be appreciative if you left a favorable review for the book on Amazon. Thank you!

Resources

Setting Boundaries – Saying No to People

Learning to say "no" to yourself and others is a very important skill to learn. Many purchases are emotionally driven, and recognizing when your emotions want to buy vs when you need something is important to having financial stability.

Martin, Sharon. (2021). The better boundaries workbook: A CBT-based program to help you set limits, express your needs, and create healthy relationships. Available on Amazon.

Tawwab, Nedra Glover. (2021). Set boundaries, find peace: A guide to reclaiming yourself. Book & separate workbook. Available on Amazon.

Finance/Investing

Being new at managing money means there is a lot to learn. After you've been budgeting for a couple of months to get comfortable tracking your money, check out some of these resources. For these websites, start with their sections on "learning more about managing money" or "learning more about investing". Don't rush through the learning process and when you are ready to invest, start slow. You've worked hard to manage your money, take your time in choosing the right investments for you.

The websites below are just a few of the many websites available where you can learn more about investing money. Explore and find the one that resonates with you.

FIRE Movement (Financial Independence, Retire Early)

Philps, Rhiannon. (January 20, 2021.) The ultimate guide to the FIRE movement. Nerdwallet. Retrieved January 31, 2024: https://www.nerdwallet.com/uk/personal-finance/guide-to-the-fire-movement/

Financial/Investing Websites

Fidelity
https://www.fidelity.com/

Dave Ramsey
https://www.ramseysolutions.com/

The Balance
https://www.thebalancemoney.com/budgeting-4074043

Investopedia Personal Finance section
https://www.investopedia.com/personal-finance-4427760

Smart About Money (The National Endowment for Financial Education) https://www.nefe.org/initiatives/smart-about-money.aspx

NerdWallet
https://www.nerdwallet.com/

Credits

Graphics:

Balance Scale: Original image by clker-free-vector-images from Pixabay modified by Diana Sturm

Bar graph: Original image by Morgan Housel from Unsplash modified by Diana Sturm

Eggs & Bread: Original image by Katrin Bolovtsova via pexels.com

Shower: Image by Ken Boyd from Pixabay.com

Shelter: Image by Noah Buscher on Unsplash

City bus: Image by Bruce Emmerling on Pixabay

Range Rover car: Image by Mike Bird on Pexels

Small kitchen: Image by Dinh Ng on Unsplash

Large kitchen: Image by Zac Gudakov on Unsplash

Web resources used:

Studio rents: Zillow. Accessed on January 27, 2024 for Manhattan, NY, NY.

Credit scores: Credit.com. (November 29, 2018). When did credit scores start? Retrieved on Jan. 28, 2024: https://www.credit.com/blog/when-did-credit-scores-start-152354/

www.ingramcontent.com/pod-product-compliance
Lightning Source LLC
LaVergne TN
LVHW021738071126
851857LV00040B/1557
* 9 7 9 8 9 9 0 0 6 8 3 0 8 *